T0195073

"HOW DO YOU FIND MALAYSIA?"

CARL JAMES

authorHOUSE®

AuthorHouse™
1663 Liberty Drive
Bloomington, IN 47403
www.authorhouse.com
Phone: 833-262-8899

Published by AuthorHouse 01/27/2021

ISBN: 978-1-6655-1548-1 (sc)
ISBN: 978-1-6655-1547-4 (hc)
ISBN: 978-1-6655-1551-1 (e)

Library of Congress Control Number: 2021901723

Print information available on the last page.

PREFACE

Can you think of an incident, perhaps a minor encounter, that monumentally changed the course of your life? Can you remember where you were, who was there, and what happened? I was 25 years old.

I was in my last semester at Central Michigan University. I had already been working through my practice teaching at Pine River High School, a consolidated school in a remote area of northern Michigan. I had also gone to have an interview at a school further south. It was a lackluster experience for both the principal and myself.

I have to confess that at this point in my life, I was a bit aimless. I spent my last summer in Michigan (I miss those summers!) working in a lakeside resort with cabins, grocery store, boats to rent, and bait and tackle. That had to be the undisputed, best summer job I have ever had. However, I was about to become aware of a fork in life's road that I had yet to recognize.

I was in the teacher's lounge at Pine River, and there was a substitute teacher there whom I had not seen before. He was maybe thirty or a bit less. He sat, relaxed, with a genial smile and one ankle rested on the opposite knee. He looked totally at rest, even though he was showing up for work in a rambunctious setting.

We chatted a bit, and I found out that he had recently returned to the United States from serving overseas in the United States Peace Corps. I went away with a strong impression that nothing could possibly faze him. I began to wonder.

I couldn't get the encounter out of my mind, so I decided to see what I could do. I had heard of the Peace Corps, of course. President Kennedy started it, and it sounded fulfilling, adventurous and life changing. I had no idea how much. I have to explain that I was not what you would call a "popular student" in school, nor was I that well known among my graduating class. I had a few very close friends, and that was my social circle. I also was not typically someone who would be likely to step outside of the stereotypical career path that a teacher might follow. I'm sure my family wondered when I was going to gain confidence, make some kind of positive direction in my life, and perhaps surprise everyone. I decided that if this is what I wanted to do, I would make sure it would happen.

I wrote and requested an application form. This was my first foray into world of National Government Officialdom and they exceeded all my foreboding expectations. I received an application form about the size of a small-town phone book. I twisted the arms of good friends to be character witnesses, and to answer questions from an agent from the FBI as they had to do a background check. I heard later that the FBI tried to weed out those who may have been agents for the CIA. The CIA presence definitely put innocent Peace Corps Volunteers in unnecessary danger. My good friends blanched but they gallantly signed up for it. That would hopefully be their first and only contact with an FBI agent.

When I was filling out my form, I came across the question, "Where would you like to serve"? Well, I hadn't given that much thought. I pondered for a bit and decided South East Asia would be a great place to go. First of all, I really did not know much other than what I had learned of the war in Viet Nam. I put down South East Asia for choice number one. I didn't take long to pick my number two. I picked The Caribbean, just because. Try growing up in Michigan with five months of snow.

In the early summer of 1977, I received my approval. I was to be a math teacher in Malaysia. The first thing I did was to look on a map and find out where Malaysia was. It seemed to be in a suitably tropical place. I learned it was nicely placed in an area that included Thailand, Indonesia, Singapore, the Philippines and the South China Sea.

I also went to the local library and borrowed a book on English grammar. My reckoning was this: the better you understood your own language, the easier it would be to learn a new one. Years later, I found out that my theory was put into practice for students learning a foreign language. I especially liked the idea of a math and English teaching assignment. I had majored in English in University, and I also minored in math. The only reason I didn't get a major in math was due to a course named "Differential Equations". That is where I bumped my head on my math ceiling.

I had never seen a passport in my entire life. So, when I received mine, I was very impressed by the seal, the formality of it, and the idea that it could take me anywhere. I figured that whatever the future held I would keep an open mind.

Now, you have to understand. I was never even close to being called a risk taker. I followed rules (until I went to University anyway) and here I was making a snap decision to leave the country for at least two years. I think my family even wondered what I was doing.

University had provided a unique and exciting experience, as I was young when I started my Freshman year. I was 17 years old. The campus was churning with anti-war protests, anti-Richard Nixon protests, ROTC protests, and anything else that riled young people up. When I arrived, there were stencils spray painted all over the campus that read, "Rubber Bob!" I had to ask. Apparently, Rubber Bob gained his moniker by chewing on pieces of rubber. I suspect there was a copious amount of LSD involved. I looked, but I never saw Rubber Bob in person.

There was also a man known as Buster who was in his mid-sixties, and rode his bicycle everywhere. I don't think he actually went to school. He just lived the campus life. He was interviewed in the campus newspaper as proudly stating that he kept his personal stash in his handlebar. Pure local color.

I got to a stage when I wasn't sure what I really wanted from university. I pulled out of CMU, and went back to my home town, Cadillac, Michigan. I shared a rental house with a good friend from high school, and worked in some unfulfilling jobs, particularly in automotive parts factories. My choices were clarified. I could drive a fork lift, or I could find something that would excite, challenge and broaden my life ahead.

Fortunately, I went back to university and finished with more determination than any I had employed, ever. All of this background of events just helped me to understand that I could actually do something different. I could do this.

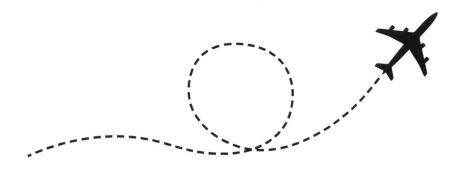

THE BEGINNING

In the year 2019 my wife and I found myself on a flight to South East Asia. For some reason, I was thinking back 42 years in the past when I made my first trip to Malaysia. Back then, I was young, wide-eyed and ready for a new experience. I had no way of comprehending exactly what lay in store for me. It was certainly beyond the limits of my imagination. Mark Twain had written a book titled, "Innocence Abroad". It was like he was referring to me.

Things were different in 1977. There was no email, facetime, text or instant messenger. Mail across the Pacific Ocean took about two weeks, so I stocked up on aerograms. They were made of ultra-light paper (like paper used by the Pony Express), that allowed space for writing on one side, and then could be folded into an envelope and then licked shut. They were much cheaper than regular mail.

My only experience out of the borders of America, up until that point in time, were two day-trips to Ontario. My departure point was at a small Traverse City airport in Michigan, on a flight first to Chicago and then to San Francisco. I was to undergo a simple orientation required by the Peace Corps.

I was really a complete hick. I spent considerable time in O'Hare Airport in Chicago trying to find out where my bags were, not knowing that they would automatically be sent on ahead to San Francisco. I had to admit I was a bit in awe when I could see San Francisco from the air in our approach. Every one of the prospective Peace Corps volunteers was quite excited when we left the airport and were shuttled to a hotel. Walking around the city was a real treat. After all, it was San Francisco in the late 1970's. It was a very different experience for one who grew up in a primarily white population. There was no doubt that SF was a multi-cultural melting pot. I was a bit dazzled by the different cultures represented there, and even looked up the corner of Haight and Ashbury. And, the Gold Dust Saloon was a favorite attraction, when we had the time.

There were sixty-five Peace Corps volunteers gathered in the city on the bay. Most were to be math or science teachers, and others were social workers. Malaysia had a severe need for help with many cases of drug addiction, and a general lack of counseling services. The need for English and math instruction was also acute.

Malaysia had obtained their freedom from the British Empire after WWII. The schools, government officials, hospitals, universities civil servants and the entire legal system relied on the English language. The government was in the midst of changing Malaysia's official language, English, back to the language of the majority people group, the Malays. It was simply called "Bahasa Malaysia".

In San Francisco, we underwent some group activities mainly to let us know how different our society was in comparison to that of Malaysia. I specifically recall one activity when everyone was divided into two groups. One was instructed to fold arms, and not accept anything. (Turned up noses were optional.)The other half was instructed to get into our personal space, smile away and graciously tried to give us presents. I think I figured out which group represented the Americans. To foreigners, we must seem to be cold, calculating and proud. Honestly, there is a smidgen of truth there.

We also had to line up and get some shots. The worst of all was a Typhoid shot. Mind you that we were about to board a flight to Hong Kong, our first stop, on the very next day. So, before we got the jab we were asked if we were right-handed or left. My laser sharp mind informed me that the normal location for the shot was going to be right in my bodily seat cushion. I had to sacrifice one of my arms. So, I rolled up my left sleeve. It wasn't too bad initially, but later, I couldn't lift my arm high enough to wash my hair for four days.

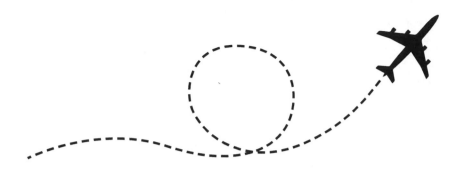

FLIGHT

Much later, in 2020, we had more of a jaded attitude towards travel to Asia. We methodically knew what to pack, what to expect and how to endure a flight of about 15 hours. Of course, we were excited to visit family, but we had no illusions about the length of the flight. You know when you are in an endurance test when you have been in the air for six hours, and you're aren't even halfway to your destination.

In 1977, we were allowed a convenient overnight stop in Hong Kong to give us time to let our bodies begin to adjust. Hong Kong in 1977 was much different than it is today. I was most struck by the appearance of the police who seemed to be out in force. They had khaki uniforms, but instead of pants they wore shorts. A very large pistol was strapped to their waist, and they looked grim enough to use them. They patrolled everywhere in pairs, with their big, black boots clopping on the sidewalks sounding like Clydesdales.

The next morning, I learned that our hotel was in Kowloon. Since we were on the mainland peninsula, many of the gang took the Star Ferry across the harbor to the island of Hong Kong. We all went sight-seeing and it was indeed eye-opening. The most immediate impression was the number of people always on the move. The most dangerous people in the city were these delivery men who pulled a large handle attached to a flat metal cart about 3 X 5 feet in size. It was the most efficient transportation system in the city. They were always in a hurry, and the metal fringe of the cart was just above the wheels, so I'm sure they fractured many ankles on a typical day. This was a city of diversity, both in population and income. Every person there appeared to be finding any way possible way to make money, and to increase what little they had.

Later in the day, we boarded Malaysian Airlines and took off for Kuala Lumpur, the capital of Malaysia. Unfortunately for those of us who were taking their first jaunt over the South China Sea, we ran into extreme turbulence, more severe than any I have experienced even until now. To put it in perspective, we nearly ran the plane completely out of alcoholic beverages.

The turbulence was so violent, we stopped the plane for a

short while on the island of Penang off the west coast of Malaysia. We had an opportunity to get out and walk around. The most intrusive environmental impact I noticed was the smell. Besides the odor of jet fuel there was a smell of compost. Not quite rotting, but pungent. Soon we boarded for our final thirty-minute leg, as the heavy clouds had moved on.

Our arrival in Kuala Lumpur was a relief. We stepped outside to get off the plane and take a bus to a terminal. The heat quickly caused our clothing to become damp, and cling to our skin. It was like we had been rolled into a hot, clammy blanket of sweat. That same ubiquitous smell discovered earlier was there also. I was able to distinguish other scents, like rotting green plants and a garden of various fruits. As we lined up for immigration and customs I was tingling with anticipation. I was desperate to get out into the city and see the country where I was contracted to work for two years.

Kuala Lumpur (meaning mud forks) is a unique city. It was, and still is, a city of contradictions. There were stunningly beautiful towering office buildings and luxury apartments. There were also small shops and food centers that looked as though they had been constructed in the 1700's. People were walking to and from work or following other pursuits like any other metropolis, but this one featured business suits, evening dresses with high heels; all the way to shorts and singlets. It must have been the peak of the fruit season because there were skins and seeds all over the sidewalks where they were casually pitched when the fruit was consumed. The most interesting fruit skin was red in color and covered with soft spines. I later learned that they were called rambutans, or "hairy".

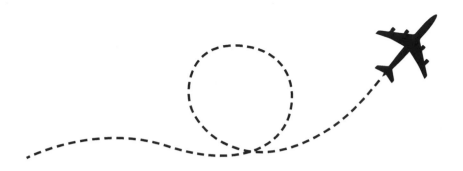

BACKGROUND

This is a good time to explain a bit of history. Back in the 1500's Arab traders were among the first visitors. Later on, the Dutch, and Jesuits and soldiers from Portugal arrived. They were explorers, traders and fortune hunters. The entire geographical area of South East Asia was known as the place to get spices. A shipload of spices in those times could mean instant retirement for the captain of the ship. The Dutch also had a presence in Indonesia. They had built a fort in Malacca, in the straits between the Malaysian peninsula and the Indonesian island of Sumatra. I have visited Malacca several times, and I am always drawn to the graveyard of the oldest church in Malaysia. The tombstones tell a story going back at least four hundred years. Entire families were wiped out by small pox. Others, struck by influenza or some other unchecked disease.

The last colonizers were the British. Their purpose of

colonization was twofold. Of course, they knew what they were doing. They helped themselves to raw materials, and engaged the local population to develop the ability to grow crops, manufacture, and trade. The British also established a school system, transportation, a legal system and a system of government; all modeled after Great Britain. They brought in immigrants from China to work in tin mines, and then they imported rubber trees from Brazil. To take care of the rubber plantations they encouraged immigrants from India to come and work there. Today, Malaysia has a vast amount of raw materials including: agriculture, palm oil, tin, rubber and petroleum.

Malaysia also suffered under Japanese occupation during WWII. The local police were tortured, and any dissenters were cruelly put to death. No one was ready for their invasion. They had an army that advanced down through the Malayan Peninsula to Singapore spurred on bicycles and each soldier with a handful of rice per day. When the war was finally over, it became clear that Malaysia (including Singapore) would become independent as the British Empire began to disintegrate.

Singapore was a poor fit for Malaysia, and planned to separate. It happened formally in 1965, only two years after Malaysia was formed. Singapore was mainly Chinese, and they had no agriculture to speak of. Their culture was different, as well as their future as they charted it. In those days, Malaysia consisted of four main ethnic groups. The native Malays formed a majority of the population, then the Chinese formed about 30%, and Indians formed about 10%. The other group consisted of Europeans and North Americans. That was a small percentage.

It was a tricky union. There was a chasm between the religious beliefs: Islam, Hinduism, Buddhism, as well as Taoism and Christianity. There was also a real variety of languages other than the national language, Bahasa Malaysia. The others were different Chinese dialects, somewhat unified by Mandarin, and a variety of Indian languages, including Tamil, Hindi, Malayalam and others.

Malaysia suffered a tragic series of events in the late 1960's. I have no idea what sparked the conflict, but terrible race riots broke out. Simplified, it was the indigenous Malays against the Chinese. It was more than just race, it was also about opportunities to advance, and the resentment of others coming into Malaysia and out earning the native population. Unfortunately, religion also got in the way unnecessarily.

No one knows how many people actually died. The capital city, Kuala Lumpur, was in a state of curfew. My future wife was a college student in Kuala Lumpur at the time, and was locked in a dormitory throughout the crisis for a long time. It was common to hear threats of murder shouted out from those outside the building.

When the situation finally eased, the government looked for ways to forge unity so that such events never occur again. They formed a united political party made up of leaders of the ethnic Malays, the Chinese and the Indians. It was called, "The National Front". This system was successful for decades, but not without some new laws that they deemed necessary to keep the peace. People could be arrested and locked up indefinitely if they started conflicts based on "sensitive issues": race, religion and the traditional rule of most states by a royal family led by a Sultan. It may sound draconian, but it achieved its purpose.

Another promotion, not a law, was that each person or family of any cultural group should celebrate traditional holidays and invite members of other races to celebrate together. So, Christmas, Chinese New Year, Hari Raya Puasa (the end of the fasting month), and Deepavali, the Indian Festival of Lights, and any others were celebrated in a community-wide environment. For a people so blessed with the gift of hospitality, it was a perfect recipe for unity.

So, into that racial and multi-cultural soup I dropped in like a housefly.

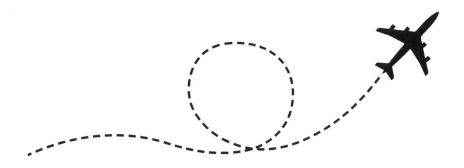

DUMB AND DUMBER

During the short stay in Kuala Lumpur, I met a good friend named Thomas. He was from Georgia, and was well stocked with very entertaining insights and expressions. My favorite was his complaint about a somewhat overanxious group leader. "He crawls up my butt like a barbed wire snake". Please insert accent if you wish. Despite our differences, he was a Southerner, and I was a Yankee; we got along very well. I did ask him once if the South had ever been able to move on after the War Between the States. He said, "No." That was it.

On a Friday night, in Kuala Lumpur, we were informed that we needed to travel on Sunday to the northern part of the country to a town called Alor Star, about thirty miles from the border with Thailand. That was where we needed to begin our eight-week course in the Malaysian national language. After that period of time, we were supposed to be skillful enough to teach high schoolers in their language.

When we were finished, we would have a couple of weeks to find out which school we were assigned to, and find lodging there.

They told us that we needed to decide on our means of travel to get up north to Alor Star, and that it would be a great experience for us. There were three very efficient ways to get there. We could get on a big long-distance bus and travel quite comfortably for six to eight hours. If we wanted a different way to travel, we could take the train. That also took a long time due to stops. The third way was the fastest, but most expensive. We could book a long-distance taxi. The taxis all seemed to be ancient Mercedes that had that distinctive engine rattle that signaled diesel fuel. Thomas and I seemed to be of one mind. None of those choices were interesting enough. We decided to leave on Saturday morning (a day early) and hitchhike. Now THAT was the way to take in some culture. It also could have been the original plot of the movie called, "Dumb and Dumber". Our plan was sketchy to say the least.

Our first challenge was to find out how to get out of Kuala Lumpur and be heading in the right direction…north. We asked around and found out that there was a bus that went out to a place called Batu Caves on the northern edge of the city. The man said the bus was either 66 or 99, he wasn't sure which. We decided that was good enough to launch a grandiose plan. We would go as far as we could on Saturday, then go to a highly recommended beach on Sunday morning, and finally complete the journey to Alor Star later that evening. It seemed foolproof. Fortunately, we remembered to give our large suitcases to a friend to take in his taxi so we weren't burdened with them.

We discovered a bus stop with plenty of information. There was a long list of bus numbers that stopped at that particular bus stop. We were in luck! Both 66 and 99 stopped there. Since 99 showed up first we clambered aboard. We may have been going in the wrong direction, or it may have been the wrong bus, but our success percentage was 25%. Good enough. As usual, we attracted several stares. I never got totally used to that. About 30 minutes later we saw a sign showing that we were near Batu Caves. That landmark signaled that we were indeed on the right path in a northern direction. So, we rang the bell and got off. We weren't ready to hitchhike yet. We saw a little coffee place so we went in, sat down and ordered tea and toast with kaya. I can't describe kaya, only to say it is creamy, sort of like coconut butter, sweet and delicious on toast.

Fully satisfied, we walked to the side of the street, stuck out our thumbs and the first car screeched to a halt. I'm not kidding. The first car. Our driver introduced himself as Timothy. He was a fairly young Chinese guy; very personable. He admitted that he stopped for us because he was curious. We had some great conversations. He told us he was traveling north to Ipoh, a town about four hours north. It was also where he grew up. It was known for the number of tin mines in the area. We decided we could break our journey there, stay the night somewhere, and continue on to the island of Penang the next day. To our surprise and delight, he took us out to eat and bought our dinner, and then took us to a Rest House. Those were clean, basic, inexpensive places to stay, similar to what we might call a hostel. After thanking him, we hit the sack.

The next morning, after a period of self-congratulations, we went out, found something to eat, and stuck out our thumbs again. It was not as fast as the day before; it took almost ten minutes to get a ride. This time our driver was a Malay man, and he was very friendly. He seemed to be motivated by kindness. Although he was somewhat quiet (he didn't speak much English), we enjoyed the ride and were able to find out little details about his family. Who doesn't want to talk about family? About halfway to Penang, we reached his turn, and we needed to get out and then hope for the next car to get us to Penang.

We were picked up, again, almost immediately. There was something about the idea of hitchhikers that must have appealed to Malaysians. The guy who picked us up drove a new Mercedes

Benz. He was Chinese, and insisted we call him "Diamond Ho". People in that part of the world seemed to think that a name was only temporary. At some time or another they just pick a name. They are not always appropriate. Once, I met a guy named "Dracula Ng," and saw the name, "Cinderella Chu", on a nametag pinned to a restaurant server. Diamond was headed to Georgetown, within a short taxi ride to the beach on Penang Island. He insisted on entertaining us with the six different horns he had installed in his car. There was the regular. Then came the police siren. Thomas and I exchanged looks. Was that legal? Is this guy nuts? Then came the Hawaii Five-O theme song. Who was this guy? Following Five-O he treated us to the 1812 Overture. I don't even remember the last two. We had heard enough. This guy was as crazy as a loon with one leg.

Finally, we reached Georgetown. We had a couple of hours to check out the beach before completing the journey. However, instead of dropping us off at the taxi stand to cross the bridge to the island, he insisted on showing us his father's scrap iron yard. We were not sure why that was an attraction, but we feigned both interest and appreciation. The big car wheeled into small lanes surrounded by piles and piles of metal. We kept seeing grubby little urchins hanging around the lane upon which we were bouncing along. Every time we met a kid, Diamond would say, "Look at my cousin! Give him the big wave!" We followed his lead. Our hand started out in the 9:00 position and slowly moved around to 3:00. We did this at least five times. I wondered how many cousins were going to appear. Mercifully, he finally took us to a taxi stand where a guy offered to take us to the beach, wait for us there, and then bring us back for 25 Malaysian Ringgit, or about five dollars. Good enough. We enjoyed the beach. If felt good to relax, and mentally rehearse what we would tell our friends. We were confident of a breathless audience. At about 6:00 or so, we went back to Georgetown. We decided that was enough hitchhiking as it was getting dark. We got into a legal taxi, and after a few wrong turns, we arrived at the hotel. I felt like Marco Polo returning to Venice. We were the first to leave Kuala Lumpur and the last to arrive in Alor Star. It was very well worth it.

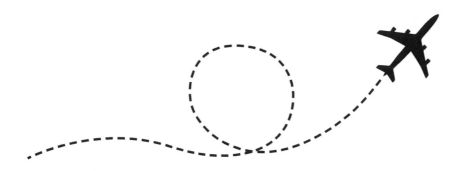

ROTI PRATA

The very next morning, our first in Alor Star, we were all assigned a bicycle. That was going to be our chief mode of transportation for the next eight weeks. At the end of that time, we were expected to step into a classroom of approximately 45 students and teach them with our incomplete command of their language. We were motivated by fear mainly. No one wants to fail; much less be humiliated by teenagers if we mispronounce words in such a way it becomes an international incident. You may think that is an exaggeration. Just wait and see. Our class schedule was 9:00 am to 4:00 pm on Monday to Friday. We also had class on Saturday from 9:00 to 12:00.

Since none of us wanted to tackle that much brain stress with an empty stomach, we set out to find a place that served breakfast. An American style breakfast was out of the question. The same rule applied to all food. We learned to never choose American food cooked in Malaysia. However, we stumbled upon something that very morning that opened a culinary door that shall never be closed. I'm talking about Roti Prata. That dish need not be capitalized, but in my mind, it is of the utmost importance. There should really be a fanfare right now.

For the entire eight-week period, I ate two rotis every morning with a large glass of freshly squeezed orange juice and strong Malaysian coffee. I will get to the coffee later.

Even to this day, after 43 years have passed, whenever I get to Singapore or Malaysia, one of my most important items on my checklist is to go out and eat roti prata. The basic ingredient is a type of dough that can be flattened out paper thin in a circle of approximately 30 inches in diameter, and about 2 mm. in thickness. The actual spreading technique is like what a pizza chef would do. The clever cook then methodically folds it over and over until there is a "pancake" of about 8-10 inches in diameter. All the while he uses generous sprinklings of lard between the layers. If done properly, it is crispy in each layer. If you ever get one that is smaller, and if it is not crispy, walk out immediately. Then the lucky customer gets them piping hot with mild curry as dipping sauce. If a picture of roti were on a Malaysian flag (and it should be) I would stand up and salute smartly with a tear in my eye. My favorite version was with egg and onions. The broken egg would be spread out so that it is between all layers, and the same procedure is for the onions. I am mildly convinced that a steady diet of roti may build up cholesterol by the bucketful, but you're only young once.

Now for the coffee. It is concocted by dumping grounds of very strong coffee locally grown in SE Asia into boiling hot water and left to brew. Then the magician (no barista here) would add sweetened, condensed milk, and pour it back and forth between two containers to make it frothy. That took skill, and no small bit of showing off. The highlight was pouring from one mug to another from a height of about three feet above the target. Not a drop was spilled. After that it would be poured into a thick china cup (it must be that kind of cup to make the experience authentic) and served. It was very strong, and the sweetness of the condensed milk balanced out any bitterness at all. I dream of Malaysian coffee.

At the time of this writing, in 2019, I was staying in my sister-in-law's home in Singapore. I strolled out of the house in the morning after our arrival, totally savoring what awaited me. The Roti shop was a 2-minute walk. The street, Jalan Kayu, was famous for 24-hour restaurants. I offered to bring back breakfast for others. As though I was doing everyone a favor. I ordered a few rotis to take back to the house, and one for me to eat while I waited. That way I got extra. That was my first taste bud guilty pleasure of the trip. Some things, thankfully, never change.

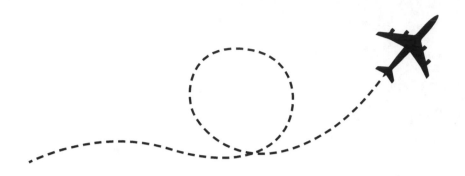

LANGUAGE

So, back in Alor Star, fortified with my obligatory sampling of culinary delights, I set off for our first day of language training. There were about 35 or so Peace Corps teachers in our group. We drew a lot of attention pedaling away down the busy streets of Alor Star. Often, we would hear a young man's voice shouting "Hey, John!" We had to experience this at least for a couple of days before we realized that we were all called John as a cultural guess, much to the disappointment of one guy named John. He thought he was a celebrity. We were also called "Mat Salleh!" I suspect that wasn't as polite as John, but it was over our heads, so we let that one go. It took about a half hour to reach the school where lessons would begin. We learned how to balance speed, breeze and the avoidance of sweat on our bicycle journey.

Since Malaysian students were not in school until January 1st the teachers were on holiday. We had a group of teachers who were highly skilled, and I suspect they were highly paid as well. They informed us right away that they were going to use the "Silent Method" of teaching. That meant that they were not going to talk at all. They would demonstrate how we use our mouth and tongue and force us to respond. Basically, we were to do all the speaking in Bahasa which was the language of the predominant ethnic group.

The teachers did not waste any time. They used elaborate exaggeration to help us work away, and we soon discovered how intense this course was going to be. We grew tired from the mental strain, and the teachers were literally sweating in their efforts to elicit some recognizable sounds from us. I can only imagine how frustrated they were to hear their language butchered like that. There were a couple of young women teaching us, and, naturally, a few guys tried to strike up non-language related conversations, but they were all politely rebuffed. These ladies had been warned. As we fought through the fog of the Bahasa vocabulary, I kept experiencing the French word popping into my mind. I had taken French for two years in High School. It was as though there was a file drawer in my brain labeled, "Language." But I kept pulling out the wrong file.

Besides official language training, we realized how important it was practice out in the streets and restaurants. We learned a very formal mode of language. Some of the first words or phrases meant "Sir" or "Uncle" or "Please Come" or Please go." It was something to hang onto, we could actually say a few phrases. Our first evening, a group of us were eating some Chinese food. There was an old man walking around between tables silently begging for money. He didn't say anything, he just stood there staring with his hand out. For a long time. Finally, one of our bolder members decided to ask the old beggar to leave him alone, because he didn't go away, and obviously wanted money. We were beginning to draw attention to ourselves. Now it's important to understand that "Please Go" was "Sila Pergi", used for formal politeness. When the annoyed diner had had enough, he spoke in a loud voice, "Sila Pergi, you old fart!" The two halves of the sentence were not at all compatible. I was kind of glad nobody understood the last part.

Even today, more than four decades later, I can still speak Bahasa well enough to have a conversation in Malaysia. My wife and I often spoke Bahasa when we didn't want our children to know what we were saying. They were very annoyed. Bahasa is also a common language also used in Singapore, and it is very similar to Indonesian and Tagalog languages.

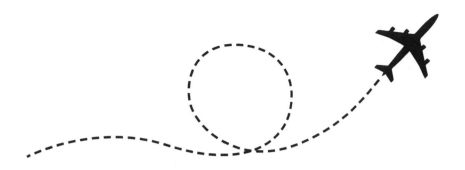

PERSONS OF INTEREST

As I started to flip through my mental calendar a few distinctive personalities begged for more attention. Staying in a small hotel, and learning in close classrooms, we got to know one another very well. My good friend, Thomas, with whom I hitchhiked, was my roommate in the hotel. Thomas had a highly developed appreciation of feminine beauty. Often, he would return to the room after walking around the city, and allowed himself to fall backwards like a domino onto his bed and stare at the ceiling. "Carl," he would say, "I have just met the most beautiful girl I've ever seen!" This scene would replay several times over the weeks ahead.

He wasn't the only one who was susceptible to charms. Another member of our group, I'll call him Dave, was besotted by a girl at the reception desk of our hotel. He would often be leaning on the counter, in a state of rapture, while she smiled (most effectively) and used her eyes to draw him under her spell. After three weeks in the hotel, he proposed marriage. We were a bit perplexed, especially given the period of courtship, and the fact that she was a Muslim, and he would have to convert to Islam. Before three days had gone by, the powers that ran the Peace Corps in Malaysia packed him up and sent him home immediately. He was no doubt upset, but I would reckon his parents appreciated their handling of the situation.

We also had a Princeton graduate in our group named Joe. His appreciation of his alma mater was on display as he wore orange pants every single day. He was also a bit of a comedian, and kept us laughing while having happy hour in the hotel lounge after our lessons were done for the day.

There was one person in our group who earned our awe and respect. Phil was assigned to teach physics at the University of Science and Agriculture. Obviously, he had had experience teaching physics at a high level. What was less obvious was the fact that he was employed as a juggler in a circus before joining the Peace Corps. He had a special backpack that contained his tools of the trade: bowling pins, balls, and many other objects that he could insert into his act. I was particularly impressed with his juggling of balls that were just a bit smaller than a tennis ball. He would practice often, and could be seen starting out with two or three balls, and work upward adding (while juggling) more and more until he could handle seven, but he had to toss them accurately at least twelve feet in the air. He was very generous with his skills; in that he would often entertain us in the hotel bar. Did I mention happy hour? It was in the sanctuary of the back of the hotel lobby. He would take a bar stool and balance it on his chin. He also bought a local umbrella made of heavy-duty paper. He would spin it and put one or two balls on it and make them stay in exactly the same spot while spinning.

If that wasn't enough, he had a photographic memory. It was sort of a barroom contest of trivia and we constantly tried to stump him. We failed miserably. One guy tried to catch him with a Charles Dickens character question. He knew the character, Stella, but never read the book. He just listened in High School. He also would share some stories.

He had a university teacher who insisted that his students HAD to take notes in class. He tried to convince the guy that he didn't need to, as he had a photographic memory. The man was inflexible. So, Phil went out and got one of those child toy drawing boards with a film over it. You could write something and make it disappear when you pulled up the film. So, the teacher had to endure the unique sound the peeling of the film produced. After all, he really was busy taking notes.

Another member of our group, Brad, was responsible for opening the door to a previously unknown delight, Indian food. Brad was a vegetarian, so he was forced to walk the streets like a detective. It was possible to get vegetarian dishes, but they were few and far between. Chinese restaurants, we learned, would use bean curd (tofu) and add enough MSG to put in a shock to our digestive system. Vince discovered a lady who had a large back patio area. She called her "restaurant" the Lakshmi House. She cooked vegetarian food served on a large banana leaf. We learned that the use of a banana leaf signified traditional food, served the right way. It was the right way all right. A bunch of us came in and there was barely enough seating to accommodate everyone. The food was served family style. We each had a banana leaf about the size of a placemat. She would come around with large kettles of different dishes, and served us generous portions. We loved it. The spice was enough to alert the brain that something was happening, yet not so spicy that the delicious taste could be overwhelmed. Much to our delight, our culinary benefactor kept coming. I think most of us had three large helpings. We were in our 20's and still ate like we were twelve. When we finished, each person had to pay the equivalent of 25 cents in US money. It was all you can eat, and I know she must have lost money. However, her delight at gaining about a dozen new converts to Indian cuisine seemed well worth the expense.

I would be amiss if I didn't share the incident of Pizza, Malaysian style. One of our group befriended a young Indian man who wanted us to go over to his house for dinner. We were kind of hoping his mom ran the Lakshmi House. That was too much to hope for.

After we were inside, he joyfully announced that he knew how much we must be missing American food. "I made you pizza!" Most of us hid our apprehension. This might not go too well. He used some kind of flatbread, similar to Chapati, and covered it with tomato ketchup and Kraft sliced cheese. Malaysia was totally devoid of "good" cheese. As we feared, it was terrible. We kept nibbling the edges, and complimented him on his cooking with false sincerity.

Providentially, he lived in a raised wooden house built on stilts. What was even better was that the city was plagued by short power outages. You guessed it, the power went out and we could see nothing, except the faint shape of the open windows. About seven pieces of Malaysian pizza sailed out like organic frisbees in all directions. Fortunately, when the lights went back on, he never suspected a thing. He pressed us to have more, but we patted our stomachs and proclaimed that we were full, thank you very much. On the way back, Thomas and I stopped for some sweet and sour pork, with rice. Thank goodness. I believed that the stray dogs took care of the evidence.

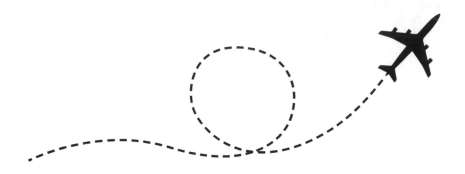

INTO THE FIRE

One day, late in our course, we were given the opportunity to actually teach a lesson to school children who were happy to come in and be taught by a group of odd, scruffy Americans. We worked in pairs so that one would observe the other. I was paired with Phil. It was a small group of students, but at least it provided us an authentic experience before the real deal. I taught an algebra lesson that wasn't terrifically challenging. These kids were brought in because they were smart. It's too bad that we thought this was a typical group scholastically. We learned better later on. My lesson was pretty forgettable, except for the time a goat wandered into the classroom, circled around and finally drifted out the door. I guess he didn't like math. Later, Phil gave me some feedback on my lesson. He only wrote this, "Get a belt". No, I didn't pack one. So, following his advice I went out that evening an bought a belt. I'm sure I was a better teacher for it.

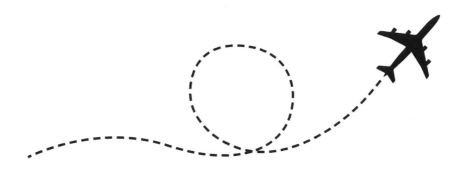

OUT AND ABOUT

Another key experience in our language training was to go out individually to a very remote village in the northern part of the country. We were to spend the weekend with a Malay family. I had newly discovered the fact that Malaysia had successfully eradicated a Communist insurgency in this area, but soon it was clear that the government took it very seriously, and they literally wrote the book on counter-insurgency. On the way to the middle of nowhere we had to stop several times at various check points. They were manned by two or three special forces types who were barricaded behind sand bags, while aiming a machine gun at us. I believe they meant business. After all, they all wore berets.

A while later our bus bounced into a small clearing with a few small buildings covered with corrugated metal. There were a couple of rickety buses in a sand lot. I followed directions and asked the driver if it was the right bus to take by using the name of the man of the house I was to visit. There was no address. He knew the name, and indicated he would stop at the right place. The moment I stepped on the bus all conversation ceased. It was like everyone pressed the mute button. As I walked to the rear of the bus, every silent face slowly rotated, like Chuckie dolls. They all seemed to be transfixed; not even breathing. I had a sudden, very irrational idea. What if I suddenly let out a scream? I could just imagine everyone bailing out the nearest window, dragging crying children along with them. I wisely decided to just sit down. Besides, that that might send the wrong message of good will in getting to know the people of Malaysia. After thrashing along on what could generously be called a road, I was informed by the driver that I was to get off. I clambered down and thanked the driver with my most engaging smile. I walked to the house hoping I could round up my meager language skills and meet my host family.

I was instructed to call the man Pacik (uncle) and the mom Macik (Auntie). One of their two sons, a teenager, greeted me in English. It turned out that he was eager to practice his English, and I wanted to practice my Bahasa. I called him Adik, which means younger brother. I kind of like the way that Malaysian people regard strangers as a family member. It is a level of community respect and closeness that we don't ordinarily have any more back in the United States. We decided to each speak in the other's language when conversing.

I dutifully handed over an envelope to Pacik that no doubt was stuffed with cash. He seemed to be very pleased. As I settled in, they asked me questions about me and my family. I responded carefully and hopefully trying not to embarrass myself. I guess I did okay because my Adik told me that Macik said I sounded like a newsreader on TV. So much for flowery language verses colloquial language. I needed to learn how to talk like ordinary people.

The next morning, I went out to watch the men tap rubber trees and gather the latex. It reminded me of people in the northern US who gathered sap for maple syrup. They created a slanted groove in the trunk of the tree, and a cup on a hook caught the milky white latex.

After walking around with Adik for most of the day, it was about 6:00. Since most people slept when it was dark, it was time for dinner. Our dinner was probably more than they were used to eating, and the envelope of cash was a big help, I'm sure. I immediately endeared myself to Macik because I really took to her cooking. Even though it was spicier than anything I was used to, I walloped it with enthusiasm. Of course, I had tears scrolling down my cheeks, my mouth was on fire, and my nose was running like a faucet, but that was a small price to pay.

After dinner, Pacik motioned for me to follow him outside. He took me to an empty cement badminton court. A crowd of men and older boys came with chairs or stools and began to circle me. I was given a chair and told to sit in the middle. I was facing a village grand jury. I overheard Pacik tell someone, "He took a picture of a tree." In my defense, it was the first rubber tree I'd ever seen.

I correctly assumed that there were no televisions there, and this was evening entertainment. They most obviously were curious about me and America, and where I lived. I must humbly say that I managed to avoid sounding like an idiot. As my confidence grew, I began a clumsy monologue of life in America, about school, family; and I tried to explain how many things that America and Malaysia had in common. I figured that we might be done for the night. Then one man asked about what was different about Malaysia compared to America. I could easily have come up with something bland, yet of interest to them. But the little imp within myself told me to have some fun. I pointed out the beautiful crescent moon in the sky. I drew their attention to it. I explained that since America was on the opposite side of the world, the crescent moon that we looked at was upside down in America. They let out breaths of awe. I was totally satisfied with the effects of my scientific expertise.

The next morning, I was walking down the road with my Adik

when an old car pulled up beside us. It was the typical car often found in remote places. It was a British make, called a "Morris Minor". It had scars that indicated a long life. The man driving was also old. Ancient in fact. From the way he was interacting with Adik, the more I realized that he was an important man in this village. I gathered very little that they said, because they talked too fast for my tender ears. Then he drove away. Adik acted like he'd been asked to tea with Queen Elizabeth. He said that I was invited to diner, and the home of the Village Head Man. He seemed to be a bit tongue-tied, and a tad jealous. I don't think there was a choice. It was a command performance.

That evening I changed into the only halfway decent clothing I packed, and walked to his house. Adik was also invited to came along, in the role of intermediary. He loved every minute of it. The Head Man was very genial, warm and polite. Even though our conversation with him was a bit unbalanced due to my mastery of the kindergarten language level, he put me at ease. He was confident, wise, and had a contentment that seemed incongruous when paired with his meager means. He also showed a level of wisdom that seemed to emanate from his smile, including his eyes. Once again, I ate fully, as that seemed to be the way to compliment the cook, and showed that I prized Malaysian food very highly. Even with my mouth on fire, I quickly accepted more food that was offered immediately when my plate was empty. I remember eating copious amounts of a dish that looked like little one-inch chopped pieces of a garden hose paired with a fiery concoction that almost strangled me. While completing my diplomatic duty, I paid verbal homage to the delicious food. Then I asked what I was eating. He smiled proudly and said, "Perut Lembu". Cow intestines. He interpreted my question as a request and piled another generous portion on my plate. I squared my shoulders back and ate it all. I reckoned that I might be on track to an ambassadorial posting considering my constantly evolving cross-cultural successes.

The next morning, I went with Adik to the little village center, back where I had boarded the bus. As we walked around, everyone wanted me to take a picture of them. Their standard pose was to stare grimly into the camera, as if getting an ID card. I didn't know why on earth they wanted me to take pictures of them. Then, I heard a loud commotion back by the buses, and saw my good friend, Thomas, arriving amid a crowd of young admirers. He had a bigger camera than I had. As we met, it felt like, "Dr. Livingston, I presume." We continued taking pictures non-stop. People on a motorcycle would stop, pose, and race off. I had no idea what they thought we should do with the pictures after they were developed.

The Kampung (village) experience was indeed valuable. The people I met were first of all very hospitable. To welcome a stranger into their home was an honor. They had very little in terms of goods, but they had a rich life with family and community that was closer than anything I had previously seen. I learned the pleasures of sitting in the yard eating pomelos taken from the tree ten feet away. If you haven't had a pomelo, you must try it tree-ripened, not from an American grocery store. They were much like a grapefruit, but larger and sweeter if taken at the right time. My horizons were much broadened over those few days.

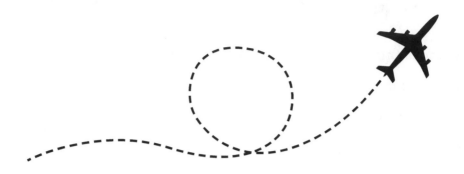

THE HIGHLANDS

There was another group-wide activity in which all Peace Corps Volunteers took part. It was a trip to a place called Genting Highlands. Yes, Malaysia had a modest mountain range like a backbone extended along the middle of the peninsula lengthwise. The altitude was about 5,000 to 6,000 feet. We were told to pack a sweater or sweatshirt for the cold. I was skeptical, but I did as I was told. The temperature was in the 50's for much of the time. It got even colder at night. It was refreshing in more ways than one.

On our trip up, we experienced quite an entertaining accident. When our bus came close to the destination, we watched as he sped rapidly toward a gantry that marked the beginning of a long driveway. As our driver was not slowing down, we leaned over to watch what was happening. Our bus was still cruising along around 40 mph when we realized that the bus was much taller than the gantry. We could do nothing but watch it get closer.

Our determined driver kept on racing along until he hit it square, right about eye level from the upper level of the bus. It was quite a satisfying crash. There is a special feeling one gets when seeing disaster approach. Wonderment was at the top of my list. How could he not see it? Besides the noise, he managed to dent the frame around the windshield, on both sides, but the window somehow remained intact. In front of us, the entire gantry toppled over, including cement moorings that had, up until that day, kept it upright. We laughed uncontrollably. One of our number managed to speak while laughing, and exclaimed, "I have to go out and see this". He stumbled down the steps and began taking photos. I don't think the driver appreciated it, but we thought it was great.

The next day I heard that there was a golf course up there. It was too good to pass up. I talked another Volunteer into joining me so we set off. We each had a caddy. Both of them were young Indian boys who seemed to be utterly unaware of any potential pitfalls along the course. For example, on one hole, I truly clobbered the ball. It went straight down the fairway where it flew over a low rise about 180 yards away. I hitched up my shorts and started to stab my club into the bag when my caddy chirped, "Lost ball".

I said, "What?"

"Lost ball," he repeated.

After further questioning, I learned there was a large hazard just over the rise. Sure enough. When I walked over the rise, I saw what looked like a swamp about thirty yards wide and about fifty yards long, and there was no way even to find the ball. I was scared of snakes as well, so I wasn't going anywhere. I don't think these caddies earned much money in tips.

Another such outing opened our eyes to a vast difference in culture. During our final days in language training, all of us (about thirty or more) booked a bus and went to a nearby "waterfall" in Kedah, the same state that contained Alor Star. We spilled out of the bus eager to see a great waterfall. I will concede this, it was very long. It also featured water running downhill at an angle of approximately 10 degrees. It was barely falling, just flowing with the gravity. There were many locals around, we saw about 10 or so couples enjoying a nice day getting their feet wet in the water. Suddenly, the wife of one of our leaders, a Japanese American, decided to take off her outer clothes and enjoy life in her bikini. In a few seconds, there were about fifty young males, newly arrived, who were definitely enjoying sights at the waterfall, while feigning no interest whatsoever. That was a bit hard to pull off. I don't know where they came from, they just appeared as though they were hiding behind rocks waiting for this moment. It was the opposite of evaporation. Word of mouth must have been fast as lightning, and no, cell phones weren't around yet.

After a while, she put her outer clothes back on and they reluctantly moved back to they were earlier. I wondered if she did that just to see the reaction. There's enough material in that incident to write a thesis.

On another occasion of having time off, I went with Ralph and Thomas on a train trip to Thailand. We didn't stop in Bangkok. It was described as a city that violated every bodily opening. We kept on chugging away to the northern part of the country to a nice little town called Chiang Mai. There were ruins from an ancient earthquake, an umbrella factory, and Batik painting (on clothing mainly) that was also very popular in Malaysia.

One day while we were there, we wanted to explore so we hired a taxi driver to take us all the way up into the Golden Triangle, which consisted of Thailand, Burma and Laos. Again, why not? On the way, we hit mud so heavy that the driver had to get out and put chains on the tires. Where I grew up those were for snow. Then we went bucking up and down on a vague pathway for what seemed to be forever. It came to us, later than it should have, that our driver could easily have robbed and killed us and no one would ever have known.

Finally, we arrived at was actually a tourist stop miles and miles from anywhere. I actually bought a postcard of lovely young maidens gathering opium poppies by the armful. I sent it to a friend. I wonder if the mail service triggered an alarm.

We hung out for a while, talked a bit with a Spaniard who was traveling the world alone, and finally we bought some souvenirs. One stood out. It was a white colored bowl, metal lining on the inside, and was called a rice bowl. Ralph asked what it was made of, and someone said "Burmese". With one or two pointed questions, we realized it was made from the top half of a Burmese skull. Thailand and Burma never liked each other much.

The next morning, we had to go to the train station and leave. The problem was, we couldn't find a taxi driver who understood us. Finally, I mimed pulling a cord, "Toot, Toot!" It worked.

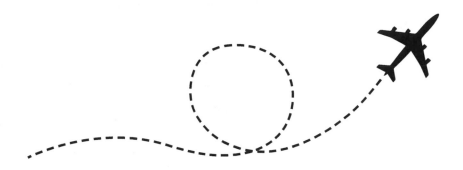

THE END OF TRAINING

Near the end of our language training, a Russian circus came to town. Since this was a backwater city nowhere close to a large affluent population, it was clear this was not the Barnum and Bailey. It didn't matter to us. A circus was a circus. It might be ratty, and the animals were a bit worn out, but we were short on entertainment. We enjoyed all that kind of schtick, and wanted to get a chance to meet some Russians. One of our guys spoke Greek from when he was an exchange student in Greece. We figured that with him armed with Greek, we could communicate effectively.

The show was just what should be expected. There was a contortionist, clowns, acrobats, a juggler, trapeze and animals that looked really sad to be there.

After the show, we met up with a few performers and our young "translator" managed to get them to agree to hanging out that evening. It was decided. We could come and meet them at their hotel. Now, this was still the Cold War era, and our immediate speculative task was to discover the identity of the KGB officer who was there to keep everyone loyal to Mother Russia. It didn't take long. The drummer for the circus band spoke very good English, and did all the talking for the others. I guess we didn't look or act like CIA agents (I silently thanked the FBI for making sure) and we were invited to participate in the consumption of vodka. We drank it Russian style. It went like this. Take a water glass, fill it with water, and cut up an onion into many slices. Take a good dollop of drink, and then suck on the onions. Repeat as often as possible. I have to believe that the end of the Cold War warmed up considerably that evening.

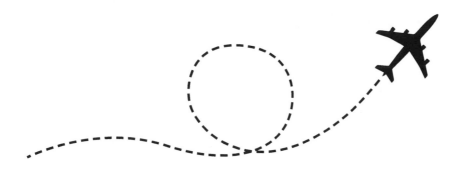

JUST AS DUMB

The time came when we had to leave Alor Star and go back to Kuala Lumpur. And, you guessed it, Thomas and I wanted to repeat our earlier hitchhiking escapade as we went back to Kuala Lumpur to get our marching orders. We didn't plan to stay overnight, just meet some more people. We found a way to get Brad to go with us, and he asked to sit in front while Thomas and I took the back seat.

We, once again, found someone to take our bags along and we would meet in the same hotel where we stayed earlier. An Indian guy stopped almost immediately, and said he was driving all the way to Kuala Lumpur. We were thinking, "Great!" Then he started questioning us about what we were doing in Malaysia. After a while we noticed that something was not quite right. He unaccountably began to act nervous. He also started driving faster as though he needed to get there as soon as possible. Since the rest of the traffic was not matching his speed, he started passing vehicles with little or no safe distance to gauge how much time we would have before getting pulverized by a logging truck. We had already heard how many times desperate drivers wanted to pass a large logging truck. Too many of them were pulverized by an approaching logging truck. These vehicles were later primarily responsible for the construction of a nationwide system of freeways.

Later, we all were hungry, and we agreed to stop and have a quick lunch. Brad was pale and wobbly, as our near brushes with death were perhaps too visible for him in the front seat. He was right where the impact would hit. Our edgy driver ordered some noodles and a pint of beer. He drank the beer in about eight seconds. We looked at each other. Why was he so worried?

Once we got on the road again, the truth came out. He cleared his throat and asked, "So, all of you Peace Corps guys are CIA, right?" We hurriedly tried to explain that they were not allowed to infiltrate the program, which also indicated that they used infiltrate freely. Thankfully, he drove a bit slower, and even was kind enough to drop us off at the hotel.

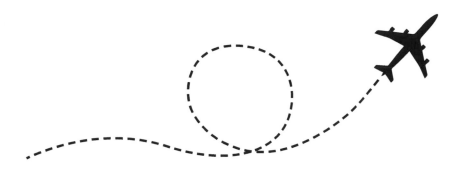

SEKOLAH SULTAN

In what seemed to be a very short time, our language training was over. We had an exam at the end of our course, and I did well, compared to the rest, but who was I kidding? The language learning curve was about to get much steeper. I was supposedly ready to go out of my relative comfort zone and teach high school math. I was assigned to a very rural school in the state of Johor. The school was named after a particular Sultan, of whom there were many in Malaysia's history. To be safe, this school is called, "Sekolah Sultan". That is the shortened version. There were about five more words in the school name. It was about a 45-minute drive inland from one of the larger cities of the state. The city was called Muar, and it was founded on the Muar River about thirty miles south of Malacca . I had the use of a hotel in Muar for a couple of weeks until I found some kind of cheap lodging. I stayed in what was one of many hotels in the country called the Great Wall Hotel. There was nothing great about it. No air conditioning, just a big ceiling fan that caused dreams of bloody dismemberment as a result of loose installation.

I learned that I was not paid by the school. I was given a Peace Corps salary that was less than half what the Malaysian teachers made. A Malaysian teacher made around 1,000 to 1,200 Ringgit per month. I made 400 per month. That was less than US$200. Self-sacrifice was part of the deal.

Almost immediately when I began working, my poverty was made public. We had an office secretary named Kamal. He oversaw all of the pay checks for each teacher. He asked me, right in front of the faculty, why I made so little compared to the others? In Malaysia, your income is everybody's business. I just told him the truth. They either figured I was very dedicated or very stupid. I think most thought the latter.

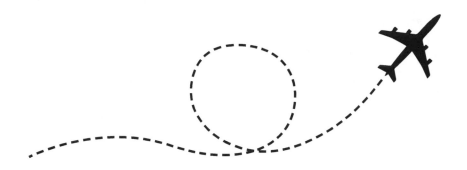

SETTLING IN

In the first few days of school a kind Chinese man named William offered me a room to stay in his house. It was roomy enough. I had a big bedroom, and I was treated like a member of the family. He was married with a little girl of pre-school age. She was very cute and shy for only about ten minutes. The family atmosphere was what I needed.

After William invited me in, he began to show me around town. He took great delight in going to dodgy places so he could point out which of his acquaintances were gangsters. Most of these places were not bars as we know them. They were restaurants that catered to a rather seamy clientele, and food was necessary only because they could pair it with alcohol. Robert instructed me on how to drink Guinness Stout. I never saw any other type of Stout all the time I was there. Just Guinness. It had to be served warm. I can only say it would have tasted better cold.

I recall one rather large and jolly individual who apparently was friends with everyone in the restaurant. He welcomed me warmly with a hefty slug on the back, and continued his heavy drinking. I noticed that a lot of big Chinese guys could drink copious amounts of alcohol with few effects, other than to increase the volume in speech, and develop a very red face. William solemnly let me know that he was an extremely dangerous man, especially if one could not pay one's debts. I see. Best to keep smiling in his presence.

William also took me to a hole in the wall eating place (I cannot call it a restaurant) that served the best dim sum in town. Dim sum is a lovely food group consisting of a large selection of delicious treats like pot stickers, dumplings, etc. It was, indeed, delicious. I became aware of the priorities of a successful restauranteur. Don't waste money on décor, or a costly piece of real estate to rent. The food always came first. People often did use expensive restaurants on special occasions, such as a wedding dinner, and that was all about "face". No one wanted to be considered cheap. I learned over time, that the owner of hole-in-the-wall restaurants took very expensive holidays over the Lunar New Year. I mean like skiing in Switzerland.

However, eating a course dinner in a fine restaurant is a great experience. When we were still in Peace Corps training, our whole group had gone to feast on a ten-course dinner. Let me be clear. It may seem, at first, that the portions are small compared to a plate in the U.S. However, try eating ten plates. Our group around the table was a bit ignorant. We dove into each course as soon as it came without realizing that the waiting staff will bring the next course immediately if you finish the current one. In our hasty greed, we were on course eight before noticing everyone else was on course four. We scored a perfect ten on appetite, but about a three on etiquette. By the way, we were absolutely stuffed.

After a few months, William told me that he would be moving house soon. I was allowed to keep the house for myself, for a pittance, as my landlady was very kind. I must say, that I did not have an indoor bathroom. That's right. I used an outdoor biffy. Every morning some poor soul at the bottom of the social hierarchy came to remove the "night soil".

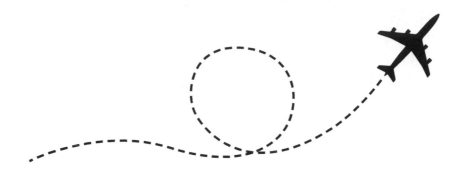

A PARANG

One of the great tragedies of my landlady's life was that her oldest son was addicted to heroin. It was only too common in those days. Petty crime was rampant, as I discovered when I lost about 40 ringgit in a jar, a camera and my favorite pair of blue jeans thanks to a burglar. It was one of the other neighbor kids who mistakenly thought the white man was rich.

My landlady was, of course, Macik to me. She was a gentle, tormented soul. One day I heard her two sons shouting in anger. I went out and learned that the older brother had stolen a boom box from his younger brother. It was typical, because he, like other addicts, would immediately sell it to get enough heroin for the day. After some general yelling, the word "thief" was shouted. The older brother went into his house and we heard something slam shut. He came out with a parang (machete). He tried to chop his brother into bits, and the younger one ran behind me for protection. He held my shoulders to ensure he would stay alive. I had no such assurance regarding my own safety. But then, William came out. He walked up to him slowly, and spoke quietly and calmly, like you would to frightened child. He then gently slid his hand down to take possession of the parang. You have no idea how relieved I was.

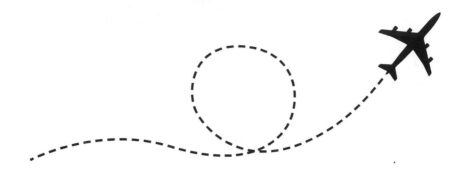

HAPPY NEW YEAR

School in Malaysia began on the first calendar day of the year. And, so it was, I began teaching on January 1, 1978. Even to this day, I always feel excitement, anticipation and not a small amount of trepidation as I contemplate the teaching year ahead. In my first teaching job, I was mostly nervous due to my shaky grasp of the language. I could just see myself making a ninny of myself by botching my lessons with embarrassing mistakes. Fortunately, I had a blackboard and chalk. Numbers are numbers, and that was what I told myself to build up confidence.

In addition to math, I was assigned to teach a couple of English classes because....I could speak it, I guess. Just imagine that of all the classes Malaysian students had to take, English was the only subject that students didn't need to pass to be able to continue their education. It did not matter. This is important because Malaysia's school system was modeled after that of Great Britain. They used the examination system. At around 8th grade, all students took an exam over all subjects. The results of this exam determined their future whether they were to enter the "Science Stream" or the "Arts Stream". Can you guess which group parents wanted their children to follow? To this day, about 90% of students and parents decide whether the student is clever or not based mainly by how they do in math. The Arts were considered a trash heap where others landed. This exam took several days, and it was the ONLY determinant for this momentous fork in the academic road. The fact that English was not considered mandatory to pass, ensured that almost no one cared about it. Another teacher (my future wife, I just didn't know it yet), had taught a complete lesson on questioning words. She spent 45 minutes going over such gems as "who, what, where, when, how, and why". At the end she decided on a short review to view her success. She erased everything and wrote the word "what" on the board. Then she asked them, "Please tell me <u>what</u> this word is." Then she repeated, "Tell me, what is this word?" One student decided to take a stab at it. He bravely shouted out, "Tell!" That kind of feedback is hard to take.

All in all, the idea that one exam influenced one's life at the junior high level was pretty scary and tense. A few years later, there is another nation-wide exam that determined whether university was possible. Again, immense pressure. My math classes were at the high school level. The math classes that I taught were either looking forward to the exam this year, or to next year. I had a curriculum that I had to complete. Oh boy. I should add here that a vast majority of my math students fully expected to fail their math exam.

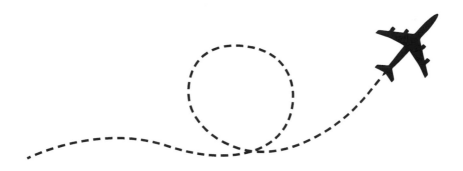

THREE BOYS

Well, that was my introduction to school in Malaysia. As informative as all of that was in helping my transition, there was a much, much bigger event that impacted me to the core. I never expected to witness something like it.

On the first day of school, all of the students were called out to a beginning of the year assembly. This group was the morning group, junior high and high school students. The younger ones had afternoon school.

They lined up militarily. The students were on a field, and an embankment considerably higher was where all the teachers sat comfortably to watch. We had chairs; the students had to stand. It was getting hot already, and it was not yet 8:00 in the morning. The students had to endure countless announcements, and rules to follow. Most of what I heard was language soup, so I was wishing for it to be over. After the Headmaster (Guru Besar) finished, the teacher in charge of discipline got up to speak. It was also tedious to listen to, and finally he finished. The Headmaster got up again and went to the microphone. Apparently, he had noticed that a few older boys in the back were talking and laughing while the discipline teacher was speaking. He called them to come up to our level. There were three of them. Not one kid was making a sound, and it was clearly apparent that no one wanted to be with these three in front of the entire student body. I looked around at the expressions on faces. Everyone except me seemed to know what was going to happen. They came up slowly, with what appeared to be intense trepidation. My sense receptors were kicking in, and I had a feeling that this was not good at all.

Our Guru Besar, a very grim man, angrily asked them a few questions. His voice got louder. The hapless boys bent their heads down and mumbled a few responses. Apparently, their responses fell short. Suddenly, without warning, he slapped each boy on the face, one after another. Their heads snapped around, and the slaps sounded like gun shots. My brain had to take a moment to catch up with my eyes. Later, I suspected this was a yearly procedure to set an example of what could happen if they stepped out of line. If I were a kid in this school, I would definitely toe the line. Always.

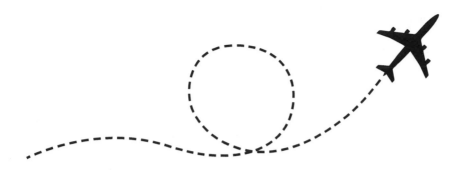

FROM A TO K

Like all other schools in Malaysia, students were steamed by ability. At the beginning of each year, every student was placed into ability groups. It was not possible for a student be in an "A" class and be in a "G" class in different subjects. There were some who were the relative elite, and others who were in the basement classes for every subject. I learned that students in the A class, spoke relatively good English, had good work habits, and were interested in learning. So it was in Sekolah Sultan where the classes ranged from the A class all the way to the K class. Unfortunately, these students at the lower rungs of the ranking ladder had very little confidence in their scholastic skills. Also, no student was ever held back to repeat a grade to help them get a better grasp of lessons. They just kept moving from year to year until they were sifted into the Arts Stream, if they didn't stop attending school altogether.

In western nations, many of the parents pushed back strongly against ability grouping in schools. It became a political issue and it was generally phased out. However, there were many parents who loved ability grouping. The only catch was that their child had to be in the top group. Otherwise, they were not happy at all. The worst outcome of ability grouping was that many students on the outside of the elite group concluded that they were dumb, and they gave up trying. Let that sink in for a moment. It is very tragic.

Malaysia was blessed with a national treasure of a cartoonist named Lat. Lat comics were required reading for the entire country. He had a regular cartoon strip in the daily papers, and he had compiled many of them into several books. Somehow, he was able to get away with making fun of those in power when ordinary citizens would not dare to do the same. He was also adept at putting his finger on little incidents that occurred in the headlines, and he would take it and apply humor. One wonderful example was that the country's legislature passed a law that a Muslim man could marry a second wife if she signed a release to allow him to do so. Immediately, there was a cartoon panel, with the image of a news headline announcing the law. The picture showed a man trying to use his wife's hand to forge her name, and apply a thumbprint on the form while she was sleeping.

He also made fun of public etiquette, like what happens when men on a bus see someone stepping aboard. He drew a few seats on a bus where each guy sat on the aisle, and no one else was by he window. If a man got on, none of the men would move. If a young lady got on board, everyone slid over to the window.

Lat even found a gold mine of ideas in the school system. He was able to find some bittersweet humor in this practice of ability grouping. He had a few panels of supposed class photos. The first photo (his drawings) showed the A class. All legs were crossed in the same direction. All hands were folded, and all were smiling warmly. The next panel was a B class, only a bit untidy, then E or F, and then the K class. The K class picture looked like an impromptu party with no plan. Lat knew his community and offered a unique point of view. Most people were able to laugh at themselves, and they appreciated his gift.

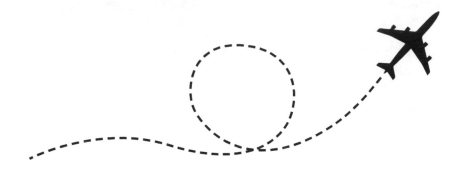

THE FACULTY LOUNGE

After a few days, I was getting by with my math lessons, and getting to know the faculty. There was a faculty lounge, which wasn't particularly comfy. There were Formica tables and plastic chairs. It was where work got done. All the students had something called "exercise books", one for each class. They did all of their classwork in those booklets, and there were forty-five students in each of my math classes. I really tried to do all the work I could in the work room. I did not want to carry anything home, especially two or three sets of those forty-five exercise books.

I soon observed that there were two social groups separated by language and religion. There was nothing acrimonious involved, people just hung with those whom they were most comfortable. There was a slight majority of ethnic Malays, the indigenous people. They spoke mostly in Bahasa, and they were all Muslims. The other group generally spoke English, and were primarily made up of two ethnic groups, Indians and Chinese. Not to mention a skinny American who didn't tilt the scales at all. This group was religiously diverse. There were Hindus, Buddhists and Christians. The good thing was that everyone got along. I noticed that the language was more of a barrier than religion was, though everyone was careful to not rock any religious boats. There were a few clever ones who could feel at ease in both groups, speaking fluently in both English and Bahasa. I aspired to that, but I never quite crossed that divide effectively. However, I really did try to get along with everyone. If they for any reason did not like me, they tactfully hid their feelings. People in Malaysia could be very polite.

As I noticed on the first day of school, there was a teacher in charge of discipline. His name was Razul. I don't know what it is about some people, but the same type will always take on jobs that give them power over others. Every classroom had a feather duster with a long rattan handle. I didn't think it was there for dusting, but for punishment. Personally, I never used one. I witnessed Razul one day yelling at a trembling little girl in the teacher's room. I gathered that she didn't do her work. She had to hold her hands out palms up while he hit them with the rattan cane. It left red welts.

On a later occasion, our Peace Corps group got together during a week off. We caught up with one another and told stories. One guy, Ralph, claimed he used the cane on some of his students and it wasn't that bad. Thomas challenged Ralph to allow him to hit him like he hit students. He agreed. One smack of the cane made him scream and jump around like he was snake-bit. All of us were thinking, "Serves him right." I suspect he changed his ways.

Often, I was asked questions by my school colleagues, mostly to satisfy their curiosity. Quite often, I even heard the question that I had been asked by many random strangers going back to the day after I arrived. "How do you find Malaysia?" I understood the particularly British origin for just such an expression, along with a few others on signs, such as "Mind your head." Every time I heard someone wonder how I found Malaysia, I wanted to say, "I went to the Philippines and turned right." I never did, though.

As I mentioned earlier, after that first day, I generally steered a bit clear of the Guru Besar. He was always polite to me, and even helpful, but I remembered the slaps and watched my p's and q's. He had a Deputy Headmaster, a man named Jamaluddin. Although Jamaluddin didn't speak English very well, he always tried to communicate with me, and he was always very friendly. Besides, it was clear to me, like most "Deputies", that he did a lot of work for the man above him. Jamaluddin was always on the move, and I judged him to be a hard-working, responsible person. Every school needs someone like Jamaluddin.

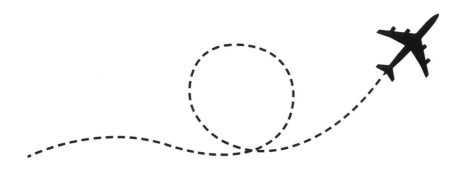

MESYUARAT

In our school, we taught the oldest students in the morning, and another team took over in the afternoon. We were done at approximately 1:00 and the afternoon crew met a bit later. Whenever we had to have a mesyuarat, or meeting, it came after we were finished and wanted to go home. It also came before the afternoon teachers had to start their classes. As a result, they asked an abundance of questions so that they could go late to class and thus shorten their day. I learned right away, most teachers in Malaysia (and I suspect more than just teachers) loved to attend meetings. I disliked meetings intensely. I felt that way especially in the heat of the afternoon, when I could be going back home, having a lunch, and taking a nice siesta.

I'll be very honest here. Ninety percent of all the meetings I have ever attended, were a significant waste of time. The real agenda could be condensed and dealt with easily and quickly. With the addition of email, there is really less reason to hold most meetings. As you can tell, this is a major pet peeve of mine.

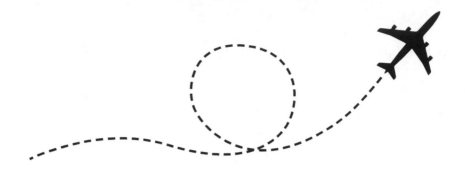

DJINNS AND BOMOHS

Jamaluddin had a wife named Zaharah. She was a key player in one of the most bizarre, and frightening, episodes I've ever experienced. The following passage will seem to be very difficult to believe.

Please understand this: everything I will write was either something I saw for myself, or witnessed by several trustworthy sources. Here we go.

Zaharah was a beautiful woman. She could walk slowly across a room and make everyone notice. I also didn't think she was particularly friendly with anyone else, especially with regard to the other women. She rarely interacted with the other ladies in the school, and seemed to be comfortable while keeping her distance. She seemed quite a bit younger than her husband, but no one knew for sure how old she was.

One day, out of nowhere, there began a series of very alarming and peculiar behaviors that turned the school upside down for a few weeks. Every time Zaharah entered a classroom, several of the teenage girls became hysterical, screamed non-stop, and ran out of the classroom like a bunch of scared rabbits. Unlike rabbits, they screamed a lot. Some were heard to shriek, "Jangan, Cikgu! Jangan, Cikgu!" (Don't, teacher!) This was almost a daily refrain, and many of us were on edge. One day, thanks to the sharp mind and fast feet of one of the afternoon teachers saved the life of a student. He ran like the wind and barely caught and grabbed a girl who was nearly run over by a truck outside the school. She had bolted from the room, and ran like a deer toward the main road. He caught her, but she fought like a marlin.

This had been going on for at least a week when the Guru Besar called in an Islamic leader, the local Imam. He sat in a chair in front of her and tried to interview her to discern what was happening. She kicked him so hard that he and the chair both went five feet backward. I saw her after that incident when I entered the work room. She sat across the room, in a chair pulled over to the wall. Even now, after more than forty years, I can still see her face. It wasn't beautiful anymore, even with the same features. She looked as cold as ice. There was a presence of evil. Her eyes were darting back and forth too fast than seemed possible. I decided I didn't need to do any work for a while and quietly excused myself from the faculty room. The Guru Besar told his deputy to take her home and keep her there until she was "better".

As women so often are able to do, many of them found out the true story. However, there was little comfort in it. Years earlier, Zaharah's grandmother went to Mecca as do many Muslims. While there, she purchased a small pouch that contained the power to keep her youth and beauty to more than stand the test of time. Just like in a Fairy Tale, there was a catch. Grandma had to let some of her blood trickle on her pouch every day. It was commonly believed to contain a Djinn that, like Rumpelstiltskin, demanded something in value in return. If she didn't faithfully feed the Djinn, or fail to pass it on to a family member before she died, she would be condemned to something far less than Paradise. The Muslim women in the school were in common agreement on this. After two weeks at home, she returned. I often checked her out of the corner of my eye, but noticed nothing out of the ordinary. If there were any further incidents, they occurred inside a circle of level of secrecy to which I did not belong.

Along similar lines, I now introduce you to the concept and existence of a "Bomoh". That is a term that enfolds the power and mystique of a Witch Doctor and also a Medicine Man. Officially, they were Practitioners of Traditional Medicine. It was puzzling to me why the local people dabbled in these things, but it was as much cultural as anything else. Bomoh's cast spells. If someone suffered from unrequited love, they could go to a Bomoh, pay some money, and go away with a small liquid potion to slip (like a Mickey Finn) into the glass of the unsuspecting future spouse. They weren't aware of what happened until after the wedding, so it is said. Before you scoff this one away completely, there is a true story of a young woman, a Peace Corps volunteer, who befell such a fate. She married a local man, and when her full faculties had returned, she immediately asked for and got an annulment. She couldn't leave the country fast enough.

When the Malaysian men's football team (soccer) had a game at the national stadium, a Bomoh would go out before the match and sprinkle powder in front of the goal mouths, to ensure that any ball that made it through belonged to the home team. Malaysia has never been to the World Cup if that's what you're wondering.

There was an article in the Malaysian national newspaper, the Straits Times, about a burglary in a nice home in Kuala Lumpur. The burglar was in the midst of gathering a real cache of valuables, until he picked up an expensive briefcase. There was a name on the briefcase; it belonged to the chief Bomoh of the country. He hurriedly put everything back, and wrote a note of apology before he left.

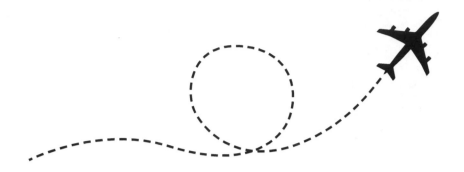

PUASA

I bring up Puasa because it was such an integral tenet of the Islam religion that affected every one of their faith. That includes the Muslim teachers and students in schools. The Puasa month required all Muslims to refrain from eating or drinking during daylight hours for one month. The purpose of this is to develop compassion for those who lack what they need to survive. People would get up around 5:00 in the morning for breakfast before the sun rose. At the end of the day, near sundown, they would prepare a big meal, and when the sun officially set, they would dig in. Considering the hot and humid climate I thought this was quite a challenge. And, in case you are wondering, no I did not try it out for a day. However, I must say that I appreciated what they were practicing. I would reckon that many of us could learn some compassion from their practice.

I think it was especially hard for outdoor laborers who were not only hungry and thirsty, they were exhausted. There were religious authorities who searched for rule breakers, and if they were caught, their photo was in the paper and they were fined. For a while I had wondered why some Chinese restaurants had seating within that was like a small room with a door. It afforded privacy for those who were particularly desperate to get something to eat, secretly.

In our school, the Muslim teachers also fasted during the fasting month. I could sympathize as they were not doubt hungry, tired and thirsty. Malaysia had very consistent weather. It was always hot, and the only variable was whether there would be rain or not. Some of the teachers would cover their face with a newspaper in the teacher's lounge, and fall asleep. If asked to enter the classroom and teach, they would sometimes say they were tired and went back to sleep. I don't think the kids got to sleep in class, though.

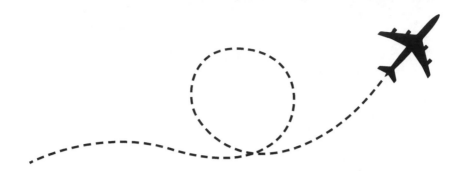

RELATIONSHIPS AND WEDDING BELLS

While all this cultural acclimation was going on, I had made some close friends. There was one in particular. She was a beautiful young Indian woman named Sara. When she smiled, her eyes flashed in a bright, wondrous way. She was highly respected in the faculty, and had apparently had survived several attempts at match-making both at school and at home. In traditional families, overzealous parents try to match their sons and daughters (particularly daughters) with an appropriate match. Looks, character and wealth were all considered with some weighted more than others, especially the projection of great wealth in the years ahead. If a man were a doctor or lawyer, he was definitely a catch.

Let's make this clear right now. I could never aspire to the level of a "catch". If I could express it metaphorically, I was the fish left in the bottom of the net to be thrown back. Not one respected matchmaker would cast me a second glance. Before coming to

Malaysia, I had cut my long (hippie) hair upon advisement from Peace Corps officials because in Malaysia it was a sign of drug use. They hanged people there. However, I still kept my Fu Manchu moustache. I was skinny, poor, and I had very little clothes sense due to an inherited condition that affected my relationship with colors like red, green and brown. I had dealt with it for years by only wearing white shirts with ties so that they didn't need to match.

As time passed, I was a frequent visitor at Sara's family home, especially around dinner time. At first, Sara's parents were very hospitable, until it dawned on them that I was interested in more than a meal. Sara's mom was definitely on my side. However, her dad was not pleased. If he had made a list of possible suitors for his daughter, I wasn't worth the price of ink to write my name. It was becoming more and more tense. When he spotted me outside the window arriving on my bicycle, he would throw the evening paper aside, mutter something derogatory, and remove himself to the sanctuary of his bedroom. The most common home-grown expression of disgust was, "Chee! Pee!"

However, the skinny, young American did not give up easily. Sara's mom and her brothers and sisters were supporters. Some of the family members decided to hatch a plan. There was a man in the Indian Community who was very much respected, especially by Sara's father. He was one of those people to whom the community brought their troubles in hopes that he could make things better. He was also blessed with calm common sense. He approached my future Father-In-Law and tried to calm him down, and let him know that his daughter still wanted to honor him, and that I was a person of character, and at least better than a thief or a murderer. Through a roundabout process of communication, Sarala's father apparently consented with grave misgivings. Sarala's mom had cornered me and said that her husband would agree if he could handle the wedding, and if I would formally ask him for her hand in marriage. I was willing, yet still nervous. I was very aware that this poor man had wanted much better for his daughter.

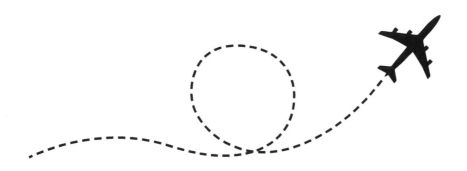

CHOLERA?

While I was living in the house on my own, I often did not bother to cook my own meals. Food was plentiful, cheap and very tasty. If I cycled into the main area of town, there were night markets with a great variety of food stalls. One of my favorites was run by an old lady who had a nice wood fire underneath a wok larger than Captain America's shield. She served the best fried noodles in town. She used flat egg noodles, vegetables, pork and cockles. It was delicious.

I also liked to go to the places that I called "point-point". I would stand in front of the glass enclosure and point out which prepared dishes I'd like to have packed up to take home. One of my favorites was an Indian Muslim place that was very popular. They served almost entirely Indian food, and I always tore into it with gusto.

One evening, after I had eaten my meal purchased from that

very restaurant, I fell very, very ill. I had a very high fever, and chills, and actually started to hallucinate going in and out of consciousness. Fortunately for me, Sara came over to my house to visit, and found me on the floor. She got a friendly neighbor to take me to the Muar Hospital, where I was able to have a consultation with a lady doctor who asked me several questions, and then announced, "I think it's cholera." I was immediately admitted in Intensive Care.

This was definitely not the Mayo Clinic. The Intensive care ward was open air, and stray cats strolled in and out with impunity. At least they kept the rodents away. After a day or two I felt a bit better, and called our Peace Corps doctor, a "Grand Dame" named Margarite who was a force of nature. She got me transferred to a private room and I was much more comfortable. When I was discharged, I still was weak, and had tons of medicine to take. Sara's father, yes, her father, insisted I come and live at their house until I was completely well.

This man was a solid believer in taking medicine on time. I would be sleeping about ten feet under when he would come and poke me awake with a bottle and spoon. He was very compassionate, and realized that I had no family. I was very grateful indeed.

Along came "Asking Day". My future father-in-law had retreated to his bedroom early. Everyone in the family was aware of what was going to happen. Brothers were whispering and laying bets on the exact time I would be bodily thrown from the room. The moment came. I went in. I asked if I could marry his daughter. I fumbled my way through my prepared speech, but maintained eye contact. Facing his worst nightmare, he very briefly explained his terms. He said yes, but we had to get married the way he wanted, an Indian wedding in a Hindu temple. I agreed, and came out relieved and triumphant. Some of the brothers probably lost money.

Before having the temple wedding ceremony, we needed to go to the Justice of the Peace to have a proper marriage certificate. Since I did not have my brother in Malaysia, I asked my good friend, Thomas, to be my best man. I was waiting with Thomas, Sarala and her mom, because her father had not yet showed up. He finally came after fortifying himself, I'm sure. It was over in just a few minutes.

The gentleman who helped broker our marriage made all the difference. Unbelievably, recently, in the summer in 2019, we had the opportunity to meet up with him in Kuala Lumpur. In his 80's, he had some memory issues, but when I reminded him who I was, and what he did for us, his memory came back. We had a good laugh, as he probably figured that our marriage was one of his greatest feats of diplomacy.

I had no idea that an event like a Hindu temple wedding could be managed with no plan whatsoever. There were a few concrete details, things to purchase, garlands of flowers to obtain, and booking the temple with a meal as well. I was left out completely on all the preparation. There was just one purchase to be made, a thali. That is similar in concept to a wedding ring (which she had), but it was a gold chain with a pendant that I needed to fasten around her neck.

On the wedding day, I was very nervous. Since I didn't have a clue what was really going to happen, I did not want to commit a public faux pas. I also realized that plenty of eyes were going to be on me, since I was the real novelty here. I entered first, decked out in a western suit. I sat cross-legged on the floor and waited. There were several women who all thought they were in charge, so they were ordering other people around most majestically. Since I had no idea what I was supposed to do, I just had to obey whatever they told me. There was no such thing as a rehearsal. The loudest voice was right.

When the bride walked in, she took my breath away. I was pretty sure at that moment no one was looking at me anymore. Together, we lit lamps, put garlands on one another, and circled the area several times while holding hands. I was reminded not to let go of her hand. I gathered that there would be dire consequences if I did. Then came the grand moment of truth. I put the thali around her neck, fastened it, and we were married. I was married! Apparently, if I had dropped the thali, it would have been a very bad omen. That didn't help my nervousness. The date was December 10th, 1978. We met in January, were dating in April, registered in September and married in December. If you're sure, don't delay.

I was sad that no one from my family could come. However, I knew my parents would understand. They got married in Kansas, my mom's home, and my grandparents on my father's side had to wait until after the wedding to meet their daughter-in-law. Her father, a hard-working farmer, was also dubious. He told his daughter that he didn't know much about this young soldier. He thought of the worst thing possible, and blurted out, "He might even be a horse thief!" Thankfully he was not. I wasn't one either.

I also realized all along that I was marrying into a very loving family. There were eleven children, with five girls first, followed by six boys. The few oldest of the girls, my wife one of them, sent a considerable amount of money every month for their family. Later, I realized they also helped the younger brothers attend University. Besides being a loving family, laughter reigned in the family home. The best time of day was around 5:00 when everyone was back at the house. There was always tea and a snack. If one was lucky enough to work in the morning, as Sara and I did, we had the pleasure of taking an afternoon nap through the heat of the day, totally setting us up for tea time. By the way, you may not think a hot drink would be welcome on a hot, muggy, afternoon. But, after a deep nap, waking up was not necessarily a quick process. I had to stare at the cup for a while, noticing how interesting the rising steam could be. Finally, I would start sipping and my mental faculties returned from some mental wasteland, brain cell by brain cell. It was a conscious change of awareness. I was, and I still am, so very grateful that I was able to take part in this daily episode of family time.

Sadly, my Father-In-Law was diagnosed with cancer not long after the wedding. He only lasted a few months, but those were good days. I was able to visit him, help relieve some pain with back rubs, and bring him things. Most visits took place using a trishaw. A great portion of the townspeople rode these often. Most rides were one or two ringgit. Like the old-fashioned rickshaw, only the "driver" pedaled a bicycle with great difficulty and dropped us off at the hospital after some crafty avoidance techniques along the busy streets. As time went on, my Father-in-Law would ask for me if someone else went to the hospital. I am grateful for those times.

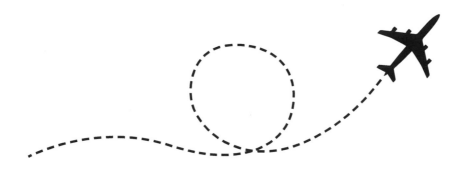

FATHERHOOD

In only a few months I found out I was to be a father. Being an expecting husband has its own unique challenges. First of all, there is no possible way I'm going to equate anything the husband does to pregnancy or childbirth. That would be silly. However, there are some interesting scenarios for the expectant father to anticipate. First, there are cravings and morning sickness. In our home, Chinese noodle soup was frequently in demand. It went down easily, and it came back out even easier. I'm so glad we had tile floors. Then there was a favorite beverage, red Fanta, called "Panta Merah". It was laced with sugar, and promoted belching. This was a fairly common evening order, so I was often charged with a vitally important errand after dark, on my trusty bicycle onto the busy streets of Muar threading my way through speeding cars to carry out my mission. There were some health issues for the mother to be, but all was good for the day when the baby would come.

February 23rd 1980 was the first day of the Year of the Monkey on the Chinese Lunar calendar. It was also the day our daughter was born. Local businesses had pooled some resources such as gift baskets for the contest to see who had the first baby in the lunar new year. Sara was in labor in the morning, and the race was on. She had been induced, and I was waiting outside with my Amah (Mom). The year of the Monkey prize was within our grasp.

Suddenly, another lady entered the delivery room, about to deliver child number ten, I think. It was then no contest. The baby came out like a kid on a water slide. The disappointment lasted about half a second. A little while later our delightful daughter was born. Ammuma (aka Grandmother) was beside herself with joy. In her world she was given a Princess. She was holding my arms and couldn't stop jumping up and down. This was her first granddaughter.

When she was little, our daughter's hair was fine, soft and somewhat blonde. Whenever we went out in public, she was the center of attention. She was quite okay with that. If we were on a bus the other passengers wanted to give her money and snacks.

There was a "confinement" period that Sara's mom had arranged for her. First off, there were daily massages to make sure everything inside was put back to where it belonged. She also had to drink essence of chicken, that contained all the nutrients of a whole chicken in a small jar. She also needed to drink brandy every day. I was just a tad jealous. When the confinement period was over, we had a regular morning routine. We lived a few hundred yards away from the family house. In the morning I would mount my bicycle. I would steer with my left hand, carry our baby with my right arm, and Sara would ride on the back, side-saddle. We were quite a sight. It felt like a circus act to me. We dropped the Princess off with her Ammuma and her Auntie much to their delight. Then we caught a ride from teaching colleagues and traveled by car to the school, about 45 minutes away.

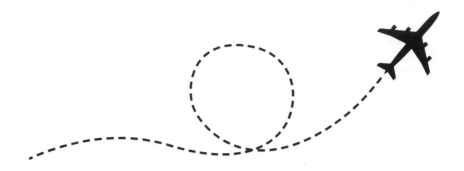

DEATH AND LOSS

This next part of our life in Malaysia is difficult to write about, even to this day. After the birth of our daughter, we had saved enough to purchase air tickets for my parents to come and visit us in Malaysia, and meet their new granddaughter. We arranged for them to come in the fall of 1980. Then I got the news that my mother suffered a severe stroke, and was not able to travel. We put the trip on hold, and entered a waiting period to see when her health would improve enough to get on a plane. I didn't have all the details, and I suspect that my family, out of kindness and concern, did not share how serious her situation actually was. So, we assumed that the following fall would work just fine.

My mom wrote and promised that she was well enough to come. I suspected later that that was not what her doctor said. I got a call on July 3rd, 1980, my parents' wedding anniversary. My mom had been talking to a distant cousin on the phone. Suddenly my mom's phone went silent. Our cousin called out several times and heard nothing. She called my younger sister who raced to the house and found her lying dead on the kitchen floor. She was only 54 years old. There was no meeting between my mom and her new granddaughter. I tried to get tickets to come to the funeral, but it was the 4th of July, and all flights were booked solid. I was broken. My Malaysian family surrounded me with love and support. Our little girl would silently stare while I cried, and she seemed to know that something was wrong. Without my wife, daughter, mother-in-law; and all brothers and sisters in Malaysia, my despair would have been hard to handle. Sara's mom, my Amah, came to me and said, "I'll be your mother as long as I will live." That meant the world to me. I also experienced the damage that occurred when closure was not possible. Years later I would uncontrollably tear up at certain moments when situations that reminded me of my mom would suddenly appear.

My dad waited a year and came by himself. When I saw him at baggage claim in the Singapore airport, I was struck by how old he looked. Shamala was a dose of delight that he needed. She was about 1 ½ years old, and she stubbornly decided that his name was "Keetum". No idea why. This was definitely a time of healing and catching up. We walked all over Muar, enjoyed food, and just enjoyed being together. Later, when we watched his plane lift off on his journey home, our little girl said, "Bye, Grandpa." Stinker.

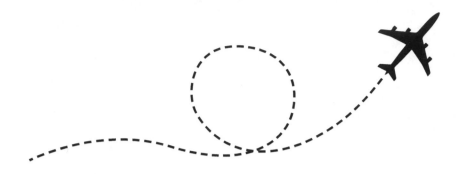

PELACUR OR PELANCUR?

Early in the year 1980, we had made long term plans to leave the Peace Corps and we decided to move to Singapore. Instead of leaving after the usual two-year term, I had extended for a third year. I would spend three complete years at the school. The entire teaching experience had affected me deeply. I carry many wonderful memories, and even today I wonder about certain students and what happened to them. I also clearly realized that I had benefited much, much more than the students and their community did as a result of my service there.

Near the end of my final year, I had a number of math students that I had taught for the entire time it took to cover the curriculum. In other words, these were the kids whom I hoped would do well on that dreaded math exam. I understood that many students were given the opportunity to advance no matter what their scores were, but I wanted to know the results anyway. After the results were received at the school, the Guru Besar, at a faculty meeting, congratulated me for the accomplishment of recording the highest percentage of the math exam passing rate in the history of the school. Under my honest and diligent effort in preparing them for an exam that could affect their lives, I waited with bated breath. The highest percentage of students to pass in the history of the school was....a whopping 20%. It took me a bit of time to understand that it really was a success. Sort of.

Not all was a glittering success as far as my teaching went. One day, I was explaining a problem that dealt with a projectile hurled into the air, and how many seconds would go by before it fell back to earth. I recited the problem, and everyone in the classroom literally fell out of their chairs laughing. I knew in my heart that my early misgivings would finally show themselves. It took a little time, but I realized the importance of the letter n. Had I said, "pelacur", all would have been well. A projectile had indeed been thrown into the air. My version had the letter "n" added. I said, "pelancur" which meant that I had thrown a prostitute into the air. The chorus of delight in my classroom probably was repeated over the dinner table that evening.

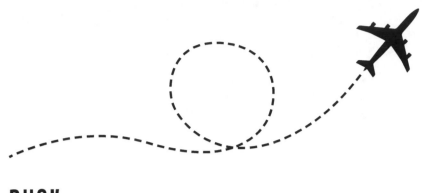

DUCK

There were so many episodes at Sekolah Sultan that deserved to be covered. We had an annual all-school sports day. Every student took part, no matter the state of their athletic ability. They were grouped into four houses, like Harry Potter, and named after historical heroes. The houses were Hang Jebat, Hang Kesturi, Hang Tuah, and hang Likiur. I was assigned to Hang Tuah. II was actually very satisfied. Apparently, he was a great warrior.

After a minimum of practice, students were randomly assigned various track and field events. There was a 100-meter dash, after which many students collapsed or threw up. There were high schoolers flinging javelins. I moved further away. I drifted further and began watching some hefty high school girls throwing a discus. This looked pretty tame. I was well off to the side of the outlines of the large sixty-degree angle of presumed flight. I heard a large roar off in the distance and I turned to see what was happening. While staring at the far away crowd I heard a chorus of desperate screams behind me. Here is the part I'll never really understand. The normal reaction was to turn around and see what was happening. Instead, I ducked. At that exact same time, I felt a discus brushing through the hair on top of my head. Only the hair. Because of that reflex, I am still living, teaching, and enjoying my family to this day. I think there was a divine prompting to duck that saved me from a cloven skull.

On the last day of school, I went from class to class to say goodbye to my students. I choked up. I had not anticipated this. They had contributed much to my experience that could not be measured. They looked at me with those big eyes and smiles, and I knew that I would never experience anything like teaching in Malaysia, ever again.

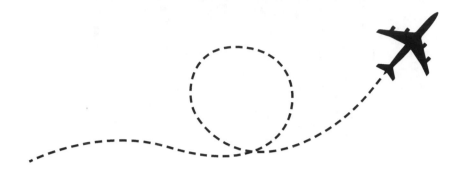

FINAL NOTES

Sarala and I talked, and confirmed our move to Singapore. There, I was not on Peace Corps pay, and we both could work for a good wage. We had already made many trips across the causeway to Singapore. It was much more developed than Malaysia was, but I'd have to say that Malaysia had more charm. Still to this day.

The Malaysian school year ended with the calendar year. The school year in Singapore schools ended in June. That gave me about six months before Sarala could resign, and we could move to Singapore. While we were excited about moving, especially not far from Sarala's home, I also felt sadness as the Peace Corps chapter of my life was closing. There were so many incidents that left a mark on me. The newspapers were filled with anecdotes that constantly reminded me that this was a unique culture that could not be duplicated anywhere.

I have often wished I had kept a journal while I was there.

There are far too many items of interest that I have forgotten. The tales in the newspapers contained such things as a tiger attack in a remote village. Rangers had to go and try to locate it and move it to a new location where it wouldn't encounter humans.

In another tale, a herd of elephants were spooked by something, and stampeded through a small village and just wreaked havoc in the lives of the poor people there. Also, in the state of Sarawak, one of the two Malaysian states on the island of Borneo, there was a crocodile that needed to go. This crocodile was estimated to be about 18 feet long, and actually earned a name, Bujang, which meant "The Bachelor". There was absolutely no similarity between this and the reality TV show of the same name. This beast had killed about 16 people over many years, and the good village people had had enough. The article went on to report that the renowned international team of "Croc Hunters" from Australia came to solve the problem. Supposedly these guys were the real deal. The last I heard, they never got him. The Bujang lived on.

Finally, the time period when I was home while Sara was still teaching provided me an extended period of time to spend with my daughter. My favorite time was feeding her breakfast in the doorway of the rear of the house where we lived. We lived in a nice little two-bedroom home with mango trees in our small front yard. In the kitchen there was a back door that opened up to an alley. Every day, an older Chinese woman would sit across the alley from us and wash her clothes in big tubs. Our girl and I provided entertainment as our neighbor tried to get her to say, "Ah-Po". I think that must have meant Grandma.

Finally, what I really got blamed for was the unfair charge of "spoiling". Sometimes little girls don't want to finish all of their food. I cleverly invented many different kinds of spoons that would finally park in her mouth. The race car spoon got there almost immediately. The airplane spoon took its time circling the landing site. My personal favorite was the helicopter spoon. It could go straight up, or down, or circle around rashly before lowering triumphantly into the expectant mouth. All the while, the helicopter made the sound; "WOP WOP WOP WOP WOP!"

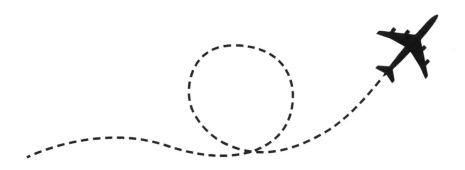

THE ISLAND

M alaysia remained, for many years, a place where our family wanted to gather together. Years later from my Peace Corps experience, the entire family, extended family, and some friends, all came along on a family reunion on an island called "Pulau Pemancing". It meant Fisherman's Island; I think. There were over thirty of us of all ages. The Island sounded beautiful. We all arrived by bus at the coastal town of Mercing. We had arranged for a large boat to take us to the island. When we took the tickets to the counter, the man said that the boat booking was canceled due to rough seas. Frankly, we didn't believe him. It wasn't that uncommon that someone hadn't done their job, the boat had been given to someone else, and they invented a story to save face. We made a fuss. We called his superior, and he told us the same story. We stubbornly stuck with our theory. We decided to wait, because it seemed very calm on shore. What made it worse was that other boats were coming and going. We asked more pointed questions, and were becoming a major nuisance to the people working there.

Finally, we were offered a boat ride to another island, where they would let off people who wanted to go there, and then the pilot agreed to take us to our destination. It was better than staying where we were, or so we thought.

Once we were a few miles off the coast, the waves were getting larger. Hmmm. After boating along for two or three hours, we let the other passengers off at their destination. Then our determined pilot fought increasingly large waves to Pulau Pemancing. Several people were very seasick by then. Finally, we arrived, and discovered two things. One, the only dock was not sheltered, and was getting hammered by the waves. Two, our pilot had no intention to let his boat get smashed. After more negotiations, he said he would take us around to the far side of the island where there was shelter from the waves. From there we could try to enlist some local fishing boats (considerably smaller) to take us to the dock. When we got there, we saw four or five boats, and figured we had it made. Unfortunately, only one boat captain volunteered to take us. His boat was licensed to carry 12 people. There were about thirty of us. We poured onto the small boat and stacked all of our luggage in the center of the boat for balance. Then, most of us lined the perimeter of the boat and locked arms. That way we could all stay on the boat, hopefully, and that also helped balance the craft.

Off we went, rolling, rising and bouncing all the way around the island back to the resort dock. Through amazing seamanship, we were able to get close enough to tie us to the dock with some slack to protect the boat. It hit the dock repeatedly, but tires roped to the sides of the craft allowed no damage. Next came the tricky ascent. The dock had no ladder, we had to grab horizontal boards nailed into place and climb up. We had a few climb up early, and they were fed all of our suitcases to pile up on the dock. There were a couple of workers on the dock helping us make sure nobody fell in, particularly between the boat and the dock as they smashed together often. These guys were small, but very strong. The two of them helped the elderly climb on their backs and carried them along as they climbed up the ladder onto the dock. Most of us just tried to time our big step with one eye of the gap between the boat and the dock. We all had a fright when my brother-in-law started to climb and slipped. He managed to catch hold again, dangled there, and made the rest of the climb. By now, wives and sisters on the dock were crying and praying. Finally, we all made it. Unbeknownst to us, a large group of guests had abandoned their dinner and were watching our progress at the railing of the restaurant, high on a hill above us. They broke out in applause and whistling when it was apparent that we all were safe.

After that, we had a great time! We did learn not to judge too quickly when we were faced with a situation that relied on listening to the experts.

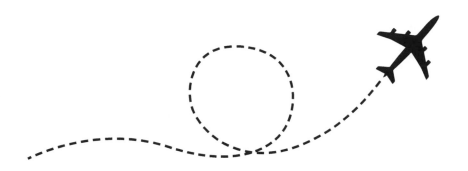

PREPARING FOR SINGAPORE

All along, I knew that a Peace Corps salary was not sustainable for our growing family. It would have been almost impossible to ask Sara to move away from her large family. At the same time, we needed to find some financial security. Our eyes were on Singapore for several reasons.

First, it was our go to place for shopping, eating, visiting friends and family, and basking in a modern city that had many amenities that Malaysia lacked. There were several family members and friends who lived there. At the same time, Singapore managed to establish its own unique culture and provided a very safe place for a family to prosper. We had visited aunts, uncles and cousins often, and it was refreshing to experience a bustling few days in a metropolis.

Long ago, Sara's first teaching assignment was in a small Malaysian town called Kulai, about 20 miles from Singapore.

She, and a friend or two from her school, often went for serious whirlwind shopping in Singapore. They would make a full day of it, and come back late at night. She knew the landscape.

Of course, nothing would happen if we didn't find jobs. Before the end of our last school year in Malaysia, employment needed to be secured. Hence, we began a serious search. Singapore had a public school system, and many private and international schools. Neither of us was interested in Singapore public schools. While teaching in Malaysia could be described as somewhat relaxed and low stress, that was not the case in Singapore. We turned our attention to private schools. We were told that a certain "College" would be a great place to apply. It was not international as others were, but it was an old trusted institution in Singapore. Before that avenue of interest could be fully explored, the owner, and founder, died. His sons were set to take over. The same people who recommended it warned us away because the sons did not measure up to the task of running a school.

After that, our search focused on schools that consisted of a wide variety of international students. Even though Singapore was small, there were at least a dozen international schools. Some of them only hired teachers with credentials from the home country. For example, there was a French School, German School, and many others that were automatically out of the question. We stumbled upon a small international school, privately owned by a British man. It was "Preparatory" in nature, and with a student body comprised with about 60 different nationalities. We started finding out necessary information and sought to set up an interview. As we were still living in Malaysia, it took some scheduling to be finalized.

Finally, we had an interview set up for the both of us. Instead of going to the school for the interview, we were invited to "The Tanglin Club". In case you are wondering, the former British colonizers still had quite a strong grip on stodgy, exclusive clubs that were very selective in their admission policies. This was intriguing; a very rare glimpse into the remnants of the British Raj.

It was exactly as we expected. Quiet, mostly male, help staff local, and well trained. It could have been a scene out of the 1930's. I expected to see W. Somerset Maugham stroll in and order a Singapore Sling. As we entered, we were "shown" to join our host. Besides the principal of the school, he was a former fighter pilot in WWII. The owner of the school was a fighter pilot in WWII. Later, I met another teacher who was, you guessed it, a fighter pilot in WWII.

He made a good pitch, and we definitely felt as though we were wanted. He kept going over the pay, and how with the both of us could be "laughing all the way to the bank". I took that with a grain of salt. Yes, schools in Singapore paid a much better salary than what we were used to having. We also clearly understood that housing in Singapore was going to be much more expensive. We were happy with our prospects, and were ready for the move.

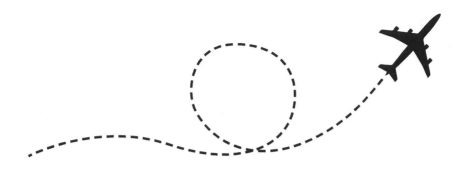

HOW DID I FIND MALAYSIA?

So, I go back to the essential question. Just how did I find Malaysia? I would like to emphasize is that Malaysia is a beautiful country, with an educated, joyful and friendly population. Kuala Lumpur is a modern metropolis that keeps local traditions and integrates the character of the country in restaurants, art and architecture. The country undergoes frequent changes in industry, tourism, and population, all while hanging on to the local color that makes Malaysia unique. Hospitality is rampant. In many ways, we never left. Sarala and I commonly speak to one another in Malay, especially when we are stalked by store employees when we are shopping. Some expressions are so unique that the English language has no worthy interpretation. There are wonderful memories of taking advantage of the resorts, food, and relative peace and tranquility. I'd have to say that we eat Malaysian food at least once or twice every week.

However, it was clear that at that time, Singapore was where our family could grow and thrive. I was sad to leave Malaysia, yet we could be back at Amah's place in just a few hours. It helped to stay nearby, and we clearly had made a good choice for the future. Some experiences claim a portion of our life that can never be usurped. If you want, fly over the Philippines from the north, turn right, and you will find Malaysia for yourself.

Printed in the United States
by Baker & Taylor Publisher Services